Taste and See

Taste and See

Prayer Services

for Gatherings of Faith

by
Jacqueline Syrup Bergan
and S. Marie Schwan

Saint Mary's Press
Christian Brothers Publications
Winona, Minnesota

With gratitude to all the men and women who,
during the past twenty years, have participated in
retreats, days of prayer, and workshops
that we have been privileged to lead.

The publishing team included Carl Koch, development editor; Jacqueline M. Captain, manuscript editor; Amy Schlumpf Manion, typesetter; inside illustrations by Vicki Shuck; cover design by Maurine R. Twait; cover photo by Wayne Aldridge, International Stock Photo; pre-press, printing, and binding by the graphics division of Saint Mary's Press.

The acknowledgments continue on page 108.

Printed in the United States of America

Printing: 9 8 7 6 5 4 3 2 1

Year: 2004 03 02 01 00 99 98 97 96

ISBN 0-88489-377-4 paper
ISBN 0-88489-391-X spiral

 Genuine recycled paper with 10% post-consumer waste.
Printed with soy-based ink.

Contents

Introduction

From the dawn of the human story, we have celebrated significant moments through ritual actions, songs, feasts, and costumes. Something deep within the human heart wants to honor the full meaning of joy and sorrow, success and failure, and the mysteries of birth and death.

Rituals employ symbols, engage our senses, and evoke our memories and emotions. Rituals tap the wellsprings of our total personality. We need rituals to discover, maintain, or renew our connection to those values that give meaning to our existence. Veterans run their fingers over a name engraved on the Vietnam Veterans Memorial in Washington, D.C., and weep. Before retiring for the night, a woman in a nursing home kisses the photo of her children. A family gathers for an evening meal. These simple rituals support, comfort, and remind us of who we are and what we believe. More elaborate rituals have the same functions.

The Christian sacramental rituals of baptism, anointing, and the Eucharist continue to celebrate the great mysteries of God's love and faithfulness. Other rituals help us celebrate diverse experiences. Each prayer service in this book incorporates a simple ritual. The rituals invite us to use all our senses in our encounters with one another and with the God who gathers us and lives among us. The rituals invite us to cherish ordinary human actions in an extraordinary way.

We hope that this collection of prayer services enhances the prayer life of Christians of all denominations. It can be used by groups or individuals.

Group Use *Taste and See* is intended primarily for groups who meet regularly for prayer, such as support groups, Christian life community gatherings, or religious communities. The prayer services or parts of them can readily be used by parish councils, staffs, faculties, and committees. Many of the prayer services can be adapted for young people.

Groups of up to ten people provide an optimal size for the intimacy of faithsharing. However, it is certainly possible to use the services with larger groups. This may change the dynamics of the sharing.

When used for a group, someone needs to assume the leader's role to preview and prepare what is needed: the setting, the materials for the rite, the music, and so on. Within an ongoing group, the leadership may alternate.

Solitary Use The prayer sessions can be used effectively by an individual for prayer. Again, it is important that the individual anticipate the time of prayer and have what is needed at hand.

Journaling is an essential component of the prayer when the services are used individually.

Elements of the Services **Setting.** Before the service begins, create a sacred space. Wherever you gather for prayer, set the tone for the service by decorating the space with candles, an open Bible, a crucifix, flowers, and so on. Particular items to help create this sacred space are listed at the end of each service in the "materials needed" section. Consult this list while planning for the service.

The following elements are included in the services:

Call to prayer. At the beginning of each service a call to prayer helps participants become centered within, quiet, focused on the particular theme, and present to God.

Prayers. Each person needs a copy of the book so that the prayers can be recited in unison, thus maximizing participation.

Reflection time. A period of five to ten minutes of silent reflection is needed to allow the Word to journey from the head to the heart. So when "reflection time" is indicated, leaders should allow that time fully.

Faithsharing. Faithsharing invites participants to express their experience of God and relationship with God. Faithsharing is not intended to be a discussion or a time to analyze or critique another's sharing. It is not appropriate to offer suggestions or advice, and confidentiality must be respected. Participants should share only what they are comfortable offering to the group.

As we share, we may be surprised that the articulation of our experience reveals new insights and enhances the experience of prayer.

To listen attentively to the faithsharing of another person is a privilege. We enter into the presence of God.

Journaling. In journaling, the pen or pencil becomes the instrument of the Spirit. Journaling opens the door to the soul. We have only to put the pen to the paper without any preconceived intent, and the Spirit within is creatively freed.

Rites. The rites are an essential component of the services. Through imagination, the use of art, gestures, music, and rituals, the theme of the prayer service and its intimate connection with the participant is concretized, symbolized, and celebrated. Incorporation of all the senses in the rites helps us celebrate with body, soul, mind, and heart.

When preparing for a group experience, the leader should try to practice the ritual beforehand so that it flows evenly. For instance, in using camphor (prayer service 21, "Fire of Love"), trying it ahead of time helps you know how much to use, how long it burns, and so on. When music and movement are used, practice helps you coordinate the two.

Music. Music plays a role in many of the prayer services. We recommend that you have available an audiocassette player or CD player. Suggested music is listed at the end of many of the prayer services. Even though we suggest a variety of music, the leader or individuals should substitute any music appropriate to the theme. If the lyrics of a recording are difficult to discern, consider having copies of the words available. When singing is called for, participants will generally need the lyrics and the music.

Other Concerns

Time. In some instances, a certain length of time for an activity is recommended. Again, be flexible. You may need to adjust the activity to fit the time available.

With some additional input, other readings based on the theme, and extended periods of time for solitary prayer and for faithsharing, some of the prayer services could conceivably be the focal point of a day or half-day of reflection.

Use of repetition. Repetition of prayers and readings sometimes occurs in the individual services. Repetition allows participants to absorb the richness of images and insights.

Resources. Having ready access to a collection of materials for use in the setting and in the rites will be helpful. This collection could include: a Bible; candles and matches; a tape player or CD player; cassettes or CDs of both instrumental and vocal music; hymnals; charcoal; incense; a censer; a cross or crucifix; doilies or runners; clay; paper; pencils; crayons; bowls and goblets; favorite pictures, icons, and statues; and an album of religious art.

Having these items readily available will facilitate preparing and creating a beautiful and meaningful setting.

We hope that these prayer services will help you share the word of God, experience the Spirit of Love more fully, and come to a deeper awareness of the unique and personal covenant to which we are all called through creation and baptism.

1
Taste and See

Be still within and without.
Prayerfully recall a moment when you
experienced the fullness of God's gifts within you.
Center yourself in God.

Call to
Prayer

Loving God,
we savor your nurturing presence
within and among us.
You fill our every hunger and need.
Grant that we may always focus on your Word
as life's sustenance and support. Amen.

Prayer

I opened my mouth;
he gave me the scroll to eat
and said,
"eat what is given to you;
eat this scroll I am giving you."
I ate it,
and it tasted sweet as honey.

(Ezekiel 3:2–3)

Reading

Reflection time

*Consider: How has the word of God nourished you? Holding
the Bible open in your lap, share how the word of God has
nourished you. If alone, write your response in your journal.*

Faith-
sharing

Rite of Bread

Play gentle instrumental music.

Read together: "'I am the bread of life. They who come to me will never be hungry'"(John 6:35). *Then pass the loaf . of sweet bread. As each person breaks off a piece, all say:* "O taste and see that Yahweh is good!" (Psalm 34:8).

Reading

I opened my mouth;
he gave me the scroll to eat
and said,
"eat what is given to you;
eat this scroll I am giving you."
I ate it,
and it tasted sweet as honey.

(Ezekiel 3:2–3)

Closing

Loving God,
we savor your nurturing presence
within and among us.
You fill our every hunger and need.
Grant that we may always focus on your Word
as life's sustenance and support.
We offer this prayer in the name of Jesus. Amen.

Setting

Materials needed. A Bible, a candle, and a loaf of sweet bread

Suggested music. Recording of gentle instrumental music, for instance, "Wings," by Michael Rowland

2
Teach Us to Pray

Be still within and without.
Center yourself in Christ.

Call to Prayer

Now once Jesus was in a certain place praying,
and when he had finished, one of the disciples said,
"Teach us to pray,
just as John taught his disciples."

(Luke 11:1)

Reading

Sing or listen to "Lord, Teach Us to Pray," by Joe Wise, or play some calming instrumental music.

Music

Gracious Jesus, as your disciples,
we, too, ask you to teach us to pray.
Deep within our heart we have a great hunger
and need for your presence and guidance.
Teach us to pray; teach us to love; teach us to live.
This we ask in your name. Amen.

Prayer

Reflection time

Consider what in the past month has been your most prayerful moment. Share this moment with one another. If alone, write your response in your journal. At the conclusion of the faithsharing or journaling, reflect silently on the gift your most prayerful moment has been for you.

Faith-sharing

Rite of Presence	*Play quieting instrumental music. Image Christ standing before you. Invite him into your soul. Absorb the light and love of Christ flowing into you. The participants who wish may pray aloud slowly, one at a time, the words, "Lord, teach us to pray."*
Reading	Now once Jesus was in a certain place praying, and when he had finished, one of the disciples said, "Teach us to pray, just as John taught his disciples." <div align="right">(Luke 11:1)</div>
Closing	*Standing in a circle, take one another's hands and pray the prayer that Jesus taught us: "Our Father . . ."*
Setting	**Materials needed.** A Bible opened to chapter 11 of Luke, a candle, and matches **Suggested music.** "Solace," by Michael Rowland, "Holy Sacred Spirit," by Monica Brown, "Lord, Teach Us to Pray," by Joe Wise

3
Thirsting for God

Be still within and without, in touch with a remembered moment of God's presence. Center yourself in God.	**Call to Prayer**
Reverently pour water into a clear glass bowl. Allow yourself to savor the sound of the water and the light reflected through it as it is poured.	
All who are thirsty, come to the water. <div align="right">(Isaiah 55:1)</div>	**Reading**
Gracious God, may your love, like water, pour over our thirsty spirits, cleansing, refreshing, renewing us. Be present as we seek to know you, to love you, and to respond to your unconditional love for us. Amen.	**Prayer**
Prayerfully read the following passages, pausing between each.	**Readings**
Like the deer that yearns for running streams, so my soul is yearning for you, my God. <div align="right">(Psalm 42:1)</div>	
All: All who are thirsty, come to the water. <div align="right">(Isaiah 55:1)</div>	

My soul is thirsting for God, the living God.
When can I enter to see the face of God?

(Psalm 42:2)

All: All who are thirsty, come to the water.

(Isaiah 55:1)

 Reflection time

Faith-sharing

Consider: What is your experience of thirst for God? Share with one another how you experience a thirst for God. If alone, write your description in your journal.

18

Play soft instrumental music.

Read together:

"If any are thirsty, let them come to me!
Let them come and drink who believe in me!"

(John 7:38)

Come forward, one at a time, and wash your hands in the water.

Rite of Water

My God, when your love spilled over
into creation
you thought of me.
I am
from love, of love, for love.
Let my heart, O God, always
recognize,
cherish,
and enjoy your goodness in all of creation.
Direct all that I am toward your praise.
Teach me reverence for every person, all things.
Energize me in your service.
Living God,
may nothing ever distract me from your
love . . .
neither health nor sickness
wealth nor poverty
honor nor dishonor
long life nor short life.
May I never seek nor choose to be other
than you intend or wish. Amen.

Closing

Materials needed. A Bible, a candle, a large clear glass bowl, a pitcher, and towels

Suggested music. Recording of soft instrumental music, for instance, "Solitude," by Michael Rowland

Setting

4

Embraced by Love

Call to Prayer

Relax in body and spirit.
Rest in God's love.
Center yourself in God.

Reading

Bystanders were bringing children to Jesus,
so that he could touch them.
When the disciples scolded them,
Jesus was indignant and said,
"Let the children come to me; don't stop them;
for the Reign of God belongs to such as these.
I say to you that anyone who does not welcome
the Reign of God like a small child will never enter it."
Then Jesus hugged the children,
and blessed them.

(Mark 10:13–16)

 Reflection time

Prayer

Loving God, Father, Mother of our being,
recall to my heart always
your tender love and faithfulness.
Like children who can look eagerly
toward their mother's kiss
and their father's embrace,
may I run freely toward your open arms,
yielding myself totally
to the joy you hold out to me. Amen.

Listen to or sing "I Have Loved You," by Michael Joncas. | **Music**

Each person should be given paper and crayons. Then let the child within you depict your yearning to be embraced by God. Share your picture with the group, particularly any feelings or insights that surprised you. If alone, write in your journal about your experience. At the conclusion of the faithsharing, silently reflect on how it has been a gift to you. | **Faith-sharing**

Play again Michael Joncas's "I Have Loved You." During the refrain, interpret the words with arm movements: | **Rite of Movement**

"I have loved you with an everlasting love": *Stretch out your arms in a gesture of embrace.*

"I have called you and you are mine": *Cross your arms over yourself in an embrace.*

May God embrace us with the peace of Jesus and send us forth strengthened by the Spirit. | **Closing**

Share a sign of peace with one another.

Materials needed. A Bible, a candle, pictures of children, a child's toy, drawing paper, and crayons | **Setting**

Suggested music. "I Have Loved You," by Michael Joncas

5
Fragrance of Love

Call to Prayer	Relax. Be quiet within and without. Become conscious of your breathing. Breathe out your distractions and darkness. Breathe in the light of God's love and presence. Breathe in . . . breathe out. . . . Center yourself in God.

Prayer

Loving God,
I declare my need for you.
You are nearer than my heartbeat,
closer than my next breath.
Gracious God,
may I always remember that
I am a cherished creature
and you are Creator. Amen.

Readings

Prayerfully read the following passages, pausing between each.

All creatures depend on you
to give them food in due season.
You give the food they eat;
with generous hand, you fill them with good things.

(Psalm 104:27–28)

All: God of Love, may I breathe in the fragrance of your being.

If you turn your face away—they suffer;
if you stop their breath—they die and return to dust.
When you give your spirit, they are created.
You keep renewing the world.

(Psalm 104:29–30)

All: God of Love, may I breathe in the fragrance of your being.

Reflection time

Recall a favorite scent. What images do you associate with this scent? Savor their memory. How does this scent speak to you of love? Share your memory with the group. If alone, write in your journal about your memory. **Faith-sharing**

Play gentle instrumental background music. Pass the fragrance around in silence. Breathe in the fragrance, savor it, and touch yourself with the scent. **Rite of Fragrance**

Give thanks to God
who always, through Christ,
gives us a role in his triumphal march.
Through us the fragrance of the knowledge of God
is being spread everywhere. **Closing**

(2 Corinthians 2:14)

Loving God, may we go forward in peace,
enjoying and spreading
the fragrance of your love. Amen.

Materials needed. A Bible, a candle, and a vial of fragrance (perfume or essential oil) **Setting**

Suggested music. "The Fairy Ring," by Michael Rowland

Note. Some people have allergic or asthmatic reactions to perfume. The leader should check with the participants to be sure that this ritual will not be harmful to anyone.

6
An Offering of Incense

Call to Prayer
Be still within and without.
Be in touch with your desire
to surrender yourself to God.
Light the incense and breathe deeply of its fragrance.
Center yourself in God.

Prayer
Loving God,
we offer all we are and have to you.
May this offering be received
as incense before you.
May all our words and actions
give you praise and glory. Amen.

Reading
I saw seven trumpets
given to the seven angels
standing in God's presence.
Another angel stood at the altar with a golden censer.
This angel was given a large amount of incense
to offer with the prayers of all the saints
on the altar of gold
that stood before the throne.
From the angel's hand
the smoke of the incense
and the prayers of the saints
went up to God's presence.

(Revelation 8:2–4)

 Reflection time

Recall as many of your ancestors as you can. Ponder each one. Among them, whom would you call "saint"? Of these, with whom would you like to join your prayer?

Share the name of one ancestor, speaking briefly of the reasons you would call her or him a "saint." After each individual shares, everyone responds with this prayer: "May your prayers and those of [name], rise like incense before God." *If you are doing this in solitude, write your responses in your journal.*

Assume a position of prayerful attentiveness before the incense.

Pray together:
To God we are the aroma of Christ,
both for those who are on the way to salvation
and for those who are on the way to destruction;
to the one the odor of death leads to death,
but to the other, the fragrance of life leads to life.
(2 Corinthians 2:15–16)

In a spirit of prayerful offering, bring to your mind and heart the ancestor with whom you identified. With your hands in a gesture of gathering, gently draw the fragrant smoke of the incense toward you. As you repeat this gesture of welcome, silently pray the above passage from 2 Corinthians again.

Sing a song of offering.

Materials needed. A Bible, incense, and a censer

Suggested music. "Take, Lord, Receive," by John Foley, "All That We Have," by Gary Ault, "Psalm 141: Incense Psalm," by Michael Joncas, or "May Christ Live in Our Hearts," by Kathy Sherman

Note. Some people have allergic or asthmatic reactions to incense. The leader should check with the participants to be sure that this ritual will not be harmful to anyone.

7
God of Goodness

Call to Prayer | Be still within and without.
Focus briefly on the "basket of goodness."
Call to your awareness God's abundant goodness to you.
Center yourself in God's goodness.

Reading | The fruits of the Spirit are
love, joy, peace, patience, kindness,
generosity, fidelity, gentleness
and self-discipline.

(Galatians 5:22–23)

Prayer | Generous God,
you are the giver of all things.
Through every single thing
we are touched with your loving presence.
Your love is everlasting,
healing and restoring us.
Your love is ever faithful,
giving courage and strength.
Your gracious love carries us,
lightening the burdens of our life.
You are our life,
the breath of our being. Amen.

Reading | The fruits of the Spirit are
love, joy, peace, patience, kindness,
generosity, fidelity, gentleness
and self-discipline.

(Galatians 5:22–23)

Reflection time

Play gentle instrumental music. Aware of how God has touched you with love, close your eyes. When you receive the basket that will be passed around, reach in, touch, and enjoy the various items in the basket. Reflect silently on how their textures speak of the various attributes and gifts of God's love.

Rite of Gifts

For some moments, imagine that you are filling a basket with all the gifts from God that you have been given. Quietly say aloud the name of the gift from God that you are most aware of at this time of your life.

Faith-sharing

If in a group, pause between each individual sharing so that the energy of gift and gratitude may penetrate the space of this gathering and each heart. If alone, write about your experience in your journal.

Sing a hymn of thanksgiving.

Closing

Materials needed. A Bible, a candle, a basket filled with various items such as a rock, twigs, gauze, satin, tweed, bark, a feather, a leaf, elastic, and so on

Setting

Suggested music. Gentle instrumental music: "We Thank You, Father," by Gregory Norbet, "Lift Up Your Hearts," by Roc O'Connor, or "All Is Gift," by Kathy Sherman

8
Seeds of New Life

Call to Prayer | Be still within and without.
Center yourself in the God of life.

Music | *Sing or listen to a hymn.*

Prayer | Gracious God,
may our deepest yearning
meet the ardent impulse
of your love and your will.
Loving God,
nourish the seed of hope
that is dormant within us.
I eagerly await the fullness of life
that only your Spirit can give.
Come, Spirit of Life. Amen.

Music | *Sing or listen to a hymn.*

Reading | Jesus said, "To what can the Reign of God be compared?
What parable can we use for it?
It is like a mustard seed; when sown in the soil,
it is the tiniest of all the seeds.
However, once it is planted
it grows into the largest shrub of all
and stretches out long branches
so that birds can dwell in its shade."

(Mark 4:30–32)

 Reflection time

Pass a small plate of mustard seeds slowly from one person to another. Take one seed and place it in the palm of your hand. As you consider the small seed, ask yourself what new life you are yearning for—that is, what within you is "waiting to be born."	**Rite of Seeds**
When you are ready, and if you feel comfortable, share briefly your desire, your yearning, that which is waiting to be born within you. Do not hurry. If you are praying alone, write your reflections in your journal or paint a picture.	**Faith-sharing**
Jesus said, "To what can the Reign of God be compared? What parable can we use for it? It is like a mustard seed; when sown in the soil, it is the tiniest of all the seeds. However, once it is planted it grows into the largest shrub of all and stretches out long branches so that birds can dwell in its shade." (Mark 4:30–32)	**Reading**
Gracious God, may our deepest yearning meet the ardent impulse of your love and your will. Loving God, nourish the seed of hope that is dormant within us. I eagerly await the fullness of life that only your Spirit can give. Come, Spirit of Life. Amen.	**Closing**
Materials needed. A Bible, a candle, a new plant, a beautiful plate of mustard seeds (available in the spice section of a supermarket), and painting supplies **Suggested music.** The refrain from "Send Us Your Spirit," by David Haas	**Setting**

9
The Cross

Call to Prayer | Be still within and without.
Focus briefly on the crucifix.
Center within yourself.

Reading | Jesus is the Beginning, the first to return from the dead,
to become supreme in all things;
for in him God wanted all fullness to be found
and to reconcile all things through him,
whether in heaven or on earth,
making peace through his death on the cross.
(Colossians 1:18–20)

 Reflection time

Prayer | Christ, risen and present,
we come, in spirit,
to stand before your cross.
The evil in human hearts
cannot stand such love as yours.
With your mother and the other disciples,
we see your love given freely.
We hope that we will respond to such love,
with great love.
Just as the rivers flow to the sea,
may all our thoughts, desires, and actions
tend toward you.
Jesus our brother,
may our hearts be filled
with an intense love for you. Amen.

Play softly as background music "Stay with Me," Laudate: Music of Taize. As the music plays, take turns holding the crucifix, reverencing it in some manner, and silently contemplating Christ's saving deeds.

Rite of Reverencing the Cross

When you are ready, and if you feel comfortable doing so, pray aloud as the Spirit may move you. If you prefer to pray silently, simply pass the cross to the next person. If alone, write your prayer in your journal.

Faith-sharing

Living God,
Jesus suffered with all of humanity
because he became "like human beings" (Philippians 2:7).
He died on the cross
because someone like Jesus who
confronts injustice,
heals the sick,
breaks the chains of oppression,
feeds the hungry,
and loves his sisters and brothers so fully
always makes enemies of tyrants and bigots,
people filled with hate.
The forces of evil cannot
tolerate such goodness.
Cleanse my soul and will of all that is destructive,
so that I can love as Jesus did,
even if it means that I too will suffer for it.
I know from Christ that death will not
have the last word.
Bring me to the glorious Resurrection,
the true victory of the cross.

Closing

Materials needed. A Bible, a candle, and a crucifix arranged on a pillow

Setting

Suggested music. "Stay with Me," *Laudate: Music of Taize*

10
Cleansing Waters

Call to Prayer Be still within and without.
Focus briefly on the bowl of water before you.
Call to your awareness the gift of your baptism.
Center yourself within God, the source of all life.

Reading In the beginning God created the heavens and the earth.
The earth had no form.
Darkness covered the face of the deep,
while a divine wind swept over the waters.

(Genesis 1:1–2)

Prayer *As you pray this prayer, extend your hands over the water.*

Loving God,
in affirmation of the inner cleansing and filling
that your love is effecting within us,
we ask your blessing
on this basic element of life—water.
Through your ever active, creative love,
may this gift of nature
be a fresh and restorative sign
of your forgiving and healing presence.
I bless this water,
drawn from the deep springs of the earth,
as a sign of cleansing and new life,
in the name of the Father
and of the Son
and of the Holy Spirit. Amen.

Jesus came from Nazareth in Galilee.
John baptized him in the Jordan River.
Just as Jesus walked out of the water,
the heavens were torn apart
and the Spirit descended on him,
in the form of a dove.
And a voice from heaven declared,
"You are my Son, my Beloved;
in you I take great delight."

(Mark 1:9–11)

Reading

Consider: What have been your experiences of water? How do these experiences speak to you of the meaning of baptism? Share the answers to these questions. Or, if you are praying alone, write your reflections in your journal.

Faith-sharing

I passed by you again and saw that
your time for love had come.
I placed my cloak over you
to cover your nakedness;
I pledged myself to you,
I entered into covenant with you
and you became mine,
says God.
Then I bathed you with water,
I washed the blood from you,
I anointed you with oil.

(Ezekiel 16:8–9)

Reading

Reflection time

Sing or listen to a hymn; then play soft background music for the rite. In memory of your baptism, immerse your hands in the blessed water. Allow your hands to remain momentarily submerged as you pray: "I renew my baptism in the name of the Father and of the Son and of the Holy Spirit." *As a sign of Christian community, allow another participant to dry your hands.*

Rite of Renewal of Baptism

Closing | This, then, is what I pray,
. . . before [God],
from whom every family,
whether spiritual or natural, takes its name:
Out of God's infinite glory,
may God give you the power through the Spirit
for your hidden self to grow strong,
so that Christ may live in your hearts
through faith,
and then, planted in love and built on love,
you will with all the saints
have strength to grasp the breadth
and the length, the height and the depth,
until knowing the love of Christ,
which is beyond all knowledge,
you are filled with the utter fullness of God.
Glory be to God
whose power, working in us,
can do infinitely more than we can ask or imagine;
glory be to God
from generation to generation
in the church and in Christ Jesus
for ever and ever. Amen.

(Ephesians 3:14–21)

Setting | **Materials needed.** A Bible, a candle, a bowl of water, and towels

Suggested music. "Song Over the Waters," by Marty Haugen, "Come to the Water," by John Foley, "Baptized in Water," by Michael Saward; background music for the rite: "Canon in D Major," by Pachelbel

11
Sprinkle Me with Hyssop

Hyssop is a healing herb symbolic of forgiveness.

Call to Prayer

Be still within and without.
Call to mind your own need for healing and forgiveness.
Center yourself in the God of mercy.

Prayer

Merciful God,
heal us of our brokenness,
purify us of our sinfulness.
As in the time of Passover
you spared the lives of your people,
spare us now, O God.
With the sprinkling of hyssop,
you released your people from death;
renew your covenant of life in us.
We pray this in the name of Jesus. Amen.

Until I am clean, bathe me with hyssop.

(Psalm 51:7)

Reading

Reflection time

In your goodness, O God, have mercy on me;
with gentleness wipe away my faults.
Cleanse me of guilt;
free me from my sins.
My faults are always before me;
my sins haunt my mind.
I have sinned against you and no other—

Reading

knowing that my actions were wrong in your eyes.
Your judgment is what I deserve;
your sentence supremely fair.

(Psalm 51:1–4)

 Reflection time

Reading | Infuse me with joy and gladness;
let these bones you have crushed dance for joy.
Please do not stare at my sins;
blot out all my guilt.
Create a pure heart in me, O my God;
renew me with a steadfast spirit.
Don't drive me away from your presence,
or take the Holy Spirit away from me.

(Psalm 51:8–11)

 Reflection time

Reading | Once more be my savior; revive my joy.
Strengthen and sharpen my still weak spirit.
And I will teach transgressors your ways;
then sinners will return to you, too.

. . . .

Sacrifices give you no pleasure;
if I offered a holocaust, you would refuse it.
My sacrifice is this broken spirit.
You will not disdain a contrite and humbled heart.

(Psalm 51:12–17)

 Reflection time

Faith-sharing | *Consider: What are the words or phrases in Psalm 51 that particularly resonate within you? What are the feelings that stir within you? Share your answers to the questions. Respond to each individual's sharing with the words: "Until I am clean, bathe me with hyssop." If alone, write your responses in your journal.*

Play "Psalm 50" and "Kyrie Eleison" from Laudate: Music *of Taize. As the hymn is playing and those who wish to are singing, all stand and bow as one of the group sprinkles the participants with the water containing the hyssop.* | **Rite of Sprinkling**

Merciful God,
heal us of our brokenness,
purify us of our sinfulness.
As in the time of Passover
you spared the lives of your people,
spare us now, O God.
With the sprinkling of hyssop,
you released your people from death;
renew your covenant of life in us. Amen. | **Closing**

Materials needed. A Bible, a candle, a bowl of water with hyssop (available through florists or local herb gardeners). If hyssop is unavailable, use a branch with small leaves in its place | **Setting**

Suggested music. "Psalm 50" and "Kyrie Eleison," *Laudate: Music of Taize*

12
Set Free

Call to Prayer	Be still within and without. Focus briefly on the chain before you. Call to mind your need to be forgiven and freed. Center yourself in God, the source of freedom.
Music	*Listen to or sing an appropriate song.*
Prayer	Christ Jesus, by your cross and Resurrection, you have set us free.
Reading	Some sat in gloom and darkness, prisoners suffering in chains for rebelling against the orders of God, for scorning the counsel of the Most High. God humbled them with hardship to the breaking point— there was no one to help them. (Psalm 107:10–12)

 Reflection time

Reading	Then they cried to Yahweh in their anguish, and Yahweh rescued them from their distress, releasing them from gloom and darkness, shattering their chains. (Psalm 107:13–14)

 Reflection time

Let them thank Yahweh for this faithful love,
for these wonderful deeds on our behalf—
breaking bronze gates open,
bursting iron bars.

(Psalm 107:15–16)

Reflection time

Christ Jesus, by your cross and Resurrection,
you have set us free.

Consider: Where in your life do you experience the lack of freedom? Do any of your life patterns (actions, habits, or attitudes) enchain you? Share one thing in your life that you experience as imprisoning you. For those praying alone, write about or draw your response.

In turn, hold the chain and take time to contemplate how it feels in your hands, its heaviness, its coldness, how the links weld it together. Contemplate the slavery that the chain symbolizes. How is the lack of freedom that you experience like the chain?

As you hold the chain, if you feel comfortable doing so, offer a spontaneous prayer asking to be released from that which holds you bound and unfree. After everyone has shared, pray together: "Christ Jesus, by your cross and Resurrection, you have set us free."

I beg of you, my Lord,
to remove anything which separates
me from you, and you from me.

Remove anything that makes me unworthy
of your sight, your control, your reprehension;
of your speech and conversation,
of your benevolence and love.

Cast from me every evil
that stands in the way of my seeing you,

hearing, tasting, savoring, and touching you;
fearing and being mindful of you;
knowing, trusting, loving, and possessing you;
being conscious of your presence
    and, as far as may be, enjoying you.

This is what I ask for myself
and earnestly desire from you. Amen.

(Peter Faber)

Music | *Sing "Amazing Grace."*

Closing | Christ liberated us.
So stand firm,
and do not submit to slavery again. (Galatians 5:1)
The fruits of the Spirit are
love, joy, peace, patience, kindness,
generosity, fidelity, gentleness
and self-discipline.
If we live by the Spirit,
let us also be led by the Spirit.

(Galatians 5:22–25)

Setting | **Materials needed.** A Bible, a candle, a cross or crucifix, a length of heavy chain, all arranged on a table, and drawing supplies

Suggested music. "Amazing Grace," by John Newton

Note. If your group does not know the history of "Amazing Grace," you might want to point out that it was written by John Newton (1725–1807). In his early life, he was an atheist and a captain of a slave ship. When he nearly died in a raging storm at sea, he had a profound experience of God. Later he embraced Christianity, wrote many beloved hymns, preached powerfully, and led the struggle against slavery.

13
Transforming Fire

Be still within and without.
Center yourself in the love of Christ.

Jesus said:
"I have come to set the earth on fire,
and I wish it were already ablaze!"

(Luke 12:49)

Place a few small pieces of paper close to the lit charcoal briquettes; there will be a short, small blaze.

Jesus said:
"I have come to set the earth on fire,
and I wish it were already ablaze!"

(Luke 12:49)

Reflection time

Consider: How is Christ a transforming fire? Recall times in your life when you have been impelled to let go of a limiting, sinful pattern of life. How was this surrender transforming, releasing you into a renewed passion for life? Share your letting go, your transformation story. If alone, write your story.

Play soft instrumental music. Pray together: "Lord, enfold me in the depths of your heart and there hold me, refine, . . . and set me on fire, raise me aloft" (Pierre Teilhard de Chardin).

As a sign of your desire to be transformed by Christ's spirit of love, do the following: On a small slip of paper, write something about you that you wish transformed with the help of God's grace. Place the paper on the live coals, praying, "Jesus, transform me by the fire of your love."

After all have placed their slips of paper on the coals, sprinkle grains of incense on the live coals and silently raise the bowl or censer in a gesture of offering.

Reading | Jesus said:
"I have come to set the earth on fire,
and I wish it were already ablaze!"

(Luke 12:49)

Closing | *Sing or listen to a final hymn.*

Setting | **Materials needed.** A Bible, a censer or bowl (lined with foil on a bed of gravel or rocks) with lit charcoal, grains of incense, matches, pencils, and a small slip of paper for each participant

Suggested music. "Titania," by Michael Rowland, "Ashes," by Tom Conry

Note. Some people have allergic or asthmatic reactions to incense. The leader should check with the participants to be sure that this ritual will not be harmful to anyone.

14
Oil of Gladness

Be still within and without.
Be aware of the need for healing in our world
as well as your personal need to be healed.
Center yourself in the healing spirit of Christ.

Call to Prayer

Listen to or sing a song.

Music

God of Blessing,
you empty us and you fill us.
Aware of the anointing of your Spirit,
we ask your blessing on this oil,
a basic gift of the earth.

Prayer

All extend one hand over the oil.

We bless this oil,
taken from the crushed olive,
as a sign of the healing love of God,
transforming, through the power of Christ,
the pain and brokenness
that is a part of each of our lives,
in the name of the Father, and of the Son,
and of the Holy Spirit. Amen.

All extend one hand over the perfume.

We bless this perfume
as a sign of the fragrance
of the Spirit of gladness
that permeates the lives of those
who know they are loved by God,

and carry within themselves
the presence of Jesus. Amen.

The oil and perfume are poured together.

Reading

Before the dawn wind rises,
before the shadows flee
I will go to the mountain of myrrh,
to the hill of frankincense.
Your name is as oil poured out,
delicate is the fragrance of your perfume.

(Song of Songs 4:6; 1:3)

**Faith-
sharing**

*Play gentle instrumental music. For the guided meditation,
close your eyes and image the healing spirit of Christ like
perfumed oil, flowing over you. . . . Envision the oil pene-
trating those parts of your body, those hurts in your heart
that are most in need of healing. . . . Feel the oil, soothing
you . . . comforting you. . . . Smell the fragrance invig-
orating you . . . energizing you. . . .*

*Share your experience of the guided meditation as far as you
are comfortable. If alone, write about the meditation in your
journal.*

Prayer

Gracious God,
soul of life and of all creation,
your healing spirit hovered over the primeval chaos,
and comes to rest over our yearnings and our desires.
Anoint us with your love,
mend our brokenness,
heal our woundedness. Amen.

**Rite of
Anointing**

*Bless one another with the oil of gladness and offer a prayer
as you do so. For example, "I bless you with the healing oil
of gladness, asking God to fill you with holy peace." If you
are praying alone, bless yourself with the oil and offer a
prayer for healing.*

44

Gracious God,   **Prayer**
send us forth into the whole world,
and let the fragrance
of your goodness and your beauty
be a sign of your love and presence. Amen.

Sing a final song.   **Closing**

Materials needed. A Bible, a candle, a small bowl of   **Setting**
olive oil, and a vial of perfumed oil or perfume

Suggested music. "Healing Is Your Touch," by Monica
Brown, "Healer of Our Every Ill," by Marty Haugen,
"Jesus, Heal Us," by David Haas, "Canon in D Major," by
Pachelbel

Note. Some people have allergic or asthmatic reactions
to perfume. The leader should check with the participants to be sure that this ritual will not be harmful to
anyone.

15
Creation

Call to Prayer	Be still within and without. Be in touch with a remembered moment of God's love. Center yourself in the creative love of God.
Prayer	My God, when your love spilled over into creation you thought of me. I am from love, of love, and for love. Let my heart, O God, always recognize, cherish, and enjoy your goodness in all of creation. Direct all that I am toward your praise. Teach me reverence for every person, all things. Energize me in your service. Living God, may nothing ever distract me from your love . . . neither health nor sickness wealth nor poverty honor nor dishonor long life nor short life. May I never seek nor choose to be other than you intend or wish. Amen.
Music	*Listen to or sing a song.*

I consider all that we now suffer does not
compare with the glory that has yet
to be revealed to us,
for all of creation eagerly awaits
for the children of God to be revealed.
Creation has been frustrated,
so that creation itself
would be freed from its bondage to corruption
and share in the same awesome liberation
as the children of God.
We know that all of creation,
has been groaning in labor pains, until now.
And not only creation, but
we, too, who have the first harvest of the Spirit,
even we are groaning inwardly,
as we anxiously await
the redemption for our bodies.

(Romans 8:18–23)

Reading

Reflection time

*Play quiet instrumental music. Mold and shape a ball of
moist clay for a while. The objective is not so much to create
something from the clay, although you may if you wish, but
to experience and enjoy the clay.*

Rite of
Clay

*Consider how you are like clay in the hands of God. What
shape does God wish for you? Reflect on your own resilience.
Share your desire to be molded and shaped by God's love
and your own resistance. Share your hopes for the future. If
alone, write your reflections in your journal.*

Faith-
sharing

Prayer   God of all creation, we ask your blessing on each of us
as we enter into the mystery
of your ongoing molding and shaping of our life.
May the spirit of Christ gift us
with the grace of loving receptivity
to your living Word
eager to be born within us.
We offer this prayer
in the name of Jesus. Amen.

Closing   *Sing a final hymn.*

Setting   **Materials needed.** A Bible, a candle, matches, a two-inch ball of moist clay for each person, a live plant, wipes for hands, paper towels, and plastic sandwich bags for taking the clay home

Suggested music. "Veni Sancte Spiritus," *Laudate: Music of Taize*, "Abba! Father!" by Carey Landry

16
Mary, Welcoming Light

Be still within and without.
Remember a moment when you walked into light.
Center yourself in the light of God's love.

Mary left for a town in Judah and
walked as quickly as possible through the hills.
When she came to Zechariah's house,
she greeted Elizabeth.
During the greeting,
the child in Elizabeth's womb leapt,
and the Holy Spirit filled her.
Giving a loud shout, she declared:
"Mary, you are the most blessed among women.
And, blessed is the child in your womb.
How do I deserve a visit
from the mother of our Lord?
From the very moment you greeted me,
my child has been leaping for joy in my womb.
Truly blessed are you who had faith
that the vow God made to you would come to fullness."
(Luke 1:39–45)

Reading

Reflection time

Loving God, radiance of our lives,
you are the light to our darkness,
hope to our despair,
promise to our dreams.
Gift our lives

Prayer

with an unfolding awareness of your life within us.
Let us live in the joyful surprise
of your transforming work,
continually creating us anew,
birthing through us,
Christ to the world. Amen.

Music | *Listen to or sing a hymn.*

Reading | The mother is the trustee of God's love to her baby. Yes, but she is even more than that, she *is* God's love to him. Giving [Mary] to him, God gives himself. (Caryll Houselander)

What a mystery it is, as unimaginable as the blessed sacrament, that Christ as man was first given God in this world by a woman! (Houselander)

[Mary] rejoiced, not first of all because she was to be the mother of God, not first of all in the sweetness of having a child of her own, but because her child was coming into the world to be light, humility, gentleness, justice, for the healing of the wounds of pride; because he who now lived in her was the world's life, and his love would prevail from generation to generation. (Houselander)

[Mary] gave birth not only to the Christ in history, but to the Christ in all of us, she gave her good simple life to be the substance of his life in us. (Houselander)

 Reflection time

Faith-sharing | *In silence, consider when you have been surprised by people who have recognized a giftedness in you, who have welcomed and affirmed you. How has this recognition and affirmation served as a light to you? Share a story that is a response to this question. If alone, write your story in your journal.*

Come forward two at a time. Light a candle and face each other. Offer each other the candle as a symbol of how we gift others with the light of Christ within us. As the candle is offered, say, "Blessed are you who believe in the promise of our God."

Hold your lighted candle during the following reading:

We must be swift to obey the winged impulses of [God's] Love, carrying him to wherever he longs to be; and those who recognize [God's] presence will be stirred, like Elizabeth, with new life. They will know [God's] presence, not by any special beauty or power shown by us, but in the way the bud knows the presence of the light, by an unfolding in themselves, a putting forth of their own beauty. (Caryll Houselander)

If alone, plan to give a candle to another person.

Listen to or sing a final hymn.

Materials needed. A Bible, a candle, a picture or icon of the meeting of Mary and Elizabeth (or, if that is unavailable, a statue of Mary or a simple statue of a woman), a small candle for each participant, and matches

Suggested music. "To My Surprise," by Rory Cooney, "Mary, Full of Grace," by Jeanne Frolick, or "Mary's Song," by Millie Rieth

Rite of Light

Closing

Setting

17
Seeking the Star

Call to Prayer	Let us be centered in Christ.
Music	*Listen to "The People That Walk in Darkness," by Bob Dufford. While the music is playing, the leader should light a candle.*
Reading	Jesus was born in Bethlehem in Judaea during the reign of King Herod. After his birth magi came to Jerusalem from the east and asked, "Where is the newborn king of the Jews? We saw his star at its rising and have come to pay him homage." <div align="right">(Matthew 2:1–2)</div>

Begin with three minutes of centering prayer: Choose a holy word or short phrase to pray silently in harmony with your breathing. You might use the name of Jesus, "Light," or the phrase "Christ, Our Light" as the prayer word. As you breathe in, silently pray "Light" or "Christ"; as you breathe out repeat "Light" or finish the phrase "Our Light."

Go on a silent, meditative procession for five to ten minutes, following the leader who carries a lighted candle. (Depending on the weather and the location, the walk may take place outside.) Conclude the meditative walk with another three minutes of centering prayer. If alone, carry the candle and make your walk.

Rite of Following the Light

I know well my plans for you,
God proclaims,
I want peace for you, not disaster,
and to give you a future full of hope.
Seek me, and you will find me;
if you search wholeheartedly.

(Jeremiah 29:11–13)

Reading

In silence, reflect on your experience of the walk. Consider how, at this time of your life, you are being called to follow the light of Christ. Share with one another the daily graces and struggles of trying to follow in Christ's light. If alone, record your reflections in your journal.

Faith-sharing

Let us faithfully go to the center with the attitude of
    the Magi,
offering to God our gold, that is,
all our false securities and the need for them.
    When you search for me you will find me;
    when you search wholeheartedly for me.
Let us faithfully go to the center with the attitude of
    the Magi,
offering to God our frankincense, that is,
all our need for controlling power
and the adulation that comes from it.

Closing

When you search for me you will find me;
when you search wholeheartedly for me.
Let us faithfully go to the center with the attitude of
the Magi,
offering to God our myrrh, that is,
all our cravings for sensual pleasures.
When you search for me you will find me;
when you search wholeheartedly for me.
Then will the star rise for us
and we, too, will come to life by a different way,
a way that will be marked by the fruits of the Spirit:
love, joy, peace, patience,
and all the other fruits of the Spirit,
as we see more and more,
in all and through all and with all,
our God and ourselves one with Him.

(Adapted from Basil Pennington)

Setting | **Materials needed.** A Bible, a candle, and matches (optional: a Christmas crèche and a candle)

Suggested music. "The People That Walk in Darkness," by Bob Dufford

18
Trust and Surrender

Be still within and without.
Center yourself in God who calls us to trust.

Call to Prayer

Sing with or listen to "Take, Lord, Receive," by John Foley. During the antiphon, the leader may lead the community in some simple repetitive gestures of offering.

Music

Take, my God, receive all of me.
Lead me into the deep trust that depends totally on you.
Gift me with the grace of surrender
that the birthing of Christ
may be realized within the reality of my everydayness.
Amen.

Prayer

Meister Eckhart speaks to us:

You can never trust God too much.
Why is it that some people do not bear fruit?
It is because they have no trust either in God or in
themselves.

Reading

Sing: Give me only your love and your grace; that's enough for me. Your love and your grace are enough for me.

Music

Julian of Norwich speaks to us:

Often our trust is not full.
We are not certain that God hears us
Because we consider ourselves worthless and as nothing.

Reading

This is ridiculous and the very cause of our weakness.
I have felt this way myself.

Music   *Sing:* Give me only your love and your grace; that's enough
for me. Your love and your grace are enough for me.

Reading   Hildegard of Bingen speaks to us:

Trust shows the way.

 Reflection time

Faith-   *Consider: In what particular area of your life are you most*
sharing   *reluctant to surrender your fears and concerns to God in*
trust? About what do you worry and feel anxious? Share
your responses with one another. If alone, write your reflec-
tions in your journal.

Prayer   Dear God, at the center of life
is the mystery of trust and surrender.
It is the heart of love,
the spring of new life and all creative effort,
and the touchstone of true freedom.
Help us join our hearts to that of the Psalmist.

Reading   Yahweh, my heart has no false pride;
my eyes do not look too high.
I am not concerned with great affairs
or things far above me.
It is enough for me to keep my soul still and quiet
like a child in its mother's arms,
as content as a child that has been weaned.
Israel, hope in Yahweh,
now and for always!

(Psalm 131)

Rite of   *Form two circles, one inside the other. The inner circle faces*
Blessing   *the outer circle. The two people face each other, join hands*
in silent blessing, then bow. The persons in the inner circle

56

move to the right and repeat the blessing gesture. The move-
ment continues until all of you have blessed one other.

Glory be to God, our Creator, to Jesus, the Christ, **Closing**
and to the Holy Spirit, who dwells in our midst,
both now and forever. Amen.

Materials needed. A Bible open to Psalm 131, a lighted **Setting**
candle, and a flower or plant

Suggested music. "Take, Lord, Receive," by John Foley

19
Called by Name

Call to Prayer

Be still within and without.
Focus briefly on the pitcher of water before you.
Call to your awareness your total dependency
on the gift of water.
Center yourself in God's goodness.

Music

Sing or listen to an opening hymn. During the music, water is slowly and reverently poured from the pitcher into the bowl.

Reading

Jesus appeared from Galilee;
he came to John at the Jordan to be baptized.
John argued with him saying,
"No, I need to be baptized by you!
Why do you come to me!"
But Jesus answered,
"Let it be like this right now;
in this way, we do what righteousness requires."
Then John consented.
After Jesus had been baptized
he walked out of the water,
and suddenly the sky opened.
The Spirit of God in the form of a dove
alighted on Jesus.
And a voice came from heaven, proclaiming
"This is my Son, my Beloved;
in him I take great delight."

(Matthew 3:13–17)

Take turns approaching the water. As each places his or her hands in the water, the community declares: "This is [name], beloved of God, whose blessings are abundant for him or her."

If you are alone, ceremonially wash your hands, praying repeatedly: "I am beloved of God, whose blessings are abundant for me."

Reflection time

Jesus, beloved of God,
you were drawn into the water of the Jordan,
draw us ever more fully into you.
Jesus, our model,
you were strengthened by the Spirit,
enliven within us
the grace and strength given to us in baptism.
Jesus, our brother,
you heard God call you "beloved,"
let those words resonate deeply within our hearts.

Add your own spontaneous intercessions.

Jesus, may all that is you flow into me.
May your body and blood
    be my food and drink.
May your passion and death
    be my strength and life.
Jesus, with you by my side
    enough has been given.
May the shelter I seek
    be the shadow of your cross.
Let me not run from the love
    which you offer,
But hold me safe from the forces of evil.
On each of my dyings
    shed your light and your love.

Rite of Naming

Prayer

Closing

Keep calling to me until that day comes,
When, with your saints,
    I may praise you forever. Amen.

(David L. Fleming)

Setting | **Materials needed.** A Bible, a pitcher of water, a bowl, and towels

Suggested music. "O Healing River," arranged by Michael Joncas

20
God's Work of Art

Be still within and without.
Be aware that you are the focus of God's creative love.
Center yourself in that love.

Call to Prayer

Gracious God,
when I consider my most loving response to you,
I am aware of the desires that you have placed deep
      within me.
You call me to be Christ in our world today.
Fulfill in me what you wish for me.

Prayer

Choose paper, pencil, crayons, or paints and spend a few minutes drawing an image that symbolically captures your dream, your deepest desire for bringing Christ within the circumstances of life.

Faith-sharing

During this time a recording of meditative instrumental music can be played as background. After approximately ten minutes, each person will have the opportunity to share his or her drawing. After the sharing, the drawings are placed on the table around the Bible.

God loved us so well that God showered us with divine mercy. Dead because of our sins, God raised us to new life through Christ. Through grace we have been saved. God raised Christ up and gave us a place in paradise in Jesus the Christ.

Reading

God did this to demonstrate the infinity of divine goodness to humanity in Christ and how infinite is God's grace. By grace we are saved through faith: not by our deeds. We cannot claim the credit. Instead, we are God's work of art, created in Christ to live the good life, just as we were meant to from creation. (Ephesians 2:4–10)

Reflection time

Rite of Blessing — *Everyone gathers around the table and extends their hands over the "dream symbols." Each person offers a spontaneous blessing over the artworks.*

Reading — We are God's work of art,
created in Christ to live the good life,
just as we were meant to from creation.

(Ephesians 2:10)

Closing — *Sing or listen to a final song.*

Setting — **Materials needed.** A Bible and a candle centered on a table, drawing paper, pencils, crayons, and paints

Suggested music. "You Are God's Work of Art," by David Haas, "Love of Us All," by Dan Schutte, or "Rest in My Wings," by Colleen Fulmer

21
Fire of Love

Be still within and without.
Center yourself in the God of love.

Call to Prayer

Jesus speaks to us:
You are a light for the world.
Let your light shine
so that everyone sees it.
Thus, when people see your good works
they will sing God's praises.

(Matthew 5:14–16)

Reading

Reflection time

Pierre Teilhard de Chardin speaks to us:

Reading

Fire, the source of being. . . . In the beginning was Power, intelligent, loving, energizing. . . . In the beginning there were not coldness and darkness: there was the Fire. . . . Blazing Spirit, Fire . . . be pleased yet once again to come down and breathe a soul into the newly formed, fragile film of matter with which this day the world is to be freshly clothed.

Ignite a small amount of camphor on a plate. In silence, contemplate the flame. The flame is carried to each of the participants. Each one holds his or her hands over the flame and when he or she feels the warmth, draws the warmth to his or her body in a gesture of blessing.

Rite of Fire

Prayer | Dearest friends,
love one another.
Remember that love comes from God.
Those who love
know God
and are children of God.

(1 John 4:7)

All: May your Word, O God, ignite within us the fire of your love.

No human has seen God.
However, if we love one another,
God dwells within us
and God's love comes to fullness in us.

(1 John 4:12)

All: May your Word, O God, ignite within us the fire of your love.

God is love.
Those who dwell in love
dwell in God,
and God in them.

(1 John 4:16)

All: May your Word, O God, ignite within us the fire of your love.

Faith-sharing | *In silence consider where, at this time in your life, are you most aware of the energy of God's love filling you and bringing you joy. A piece of camphor is lit. Form a circle around the fire. Each person is invited to speak spontaneously a word or phrase from the Scriptures that expresses for them an energizing assurance of God's love. After each person speaks, all respond with "Your Word, O God, is light, warmth, and life." If praying alone, write your response in your journal.*

My God, when your love spilled over
into creation
you thought of me.
I am
from love, of love, for love.
Let my heart, O God, always
recognize,
cherish,
and enjoy your goodness in all of creation.
Direct all that I am toward your praise.
Teach me reverence for every person, all things.
Energize me in your service.
Living God,
may nothing ever distract me from your
love . . .
neither health nor sickness
wealth nor poverty
honor nor dishonor
long life nor short life.
May I never seek nor choose to be other
than you intend or wish. Amen.

Materials needed. A Bible, a stand with a heat-resistant plate for flame, camphor (available from a pharmacy), and matches

Note. It is essential that before the prayer service the leader practice lighting the camphor in order to determine the size of the piece of camphor to be used and the timing of lighting it.

Note. Some people have allergic or asthmatic reactions to burning camphor. The leader should check with the participants to be sure that this ritual will not be harmful to anyone.

22
Anointed in Compassion

Call to Prayer | Be still within and without.
Center yourself in the compassion of Christ.

Music | *Sing or listen to a hymn.*

Reading | Jesus returned to Nazareth where he had been raised
and entered the synagogue
as he regularly did on the Sabbath.
When he rose to read,
they gave him the scroll for Isaiah, the prophet.
He unrolled it and read this passage:
"God's spirit is in me,
because God has anointed me
to carry the Good News to those who are afflicted.
God has sent me to declare freedom to prisoners,
vision to the blind, and liberation to the oppressed."
Then Jesus rolled up the scroll,
returned it, and took his seat.
Everyone in the synagogue stared at him.
Jesus said for all to hear:
"This prophecy is being fulfilled right now,
even as you listen."

(Luke 4:16–21)

 Reflection time

Faith-sharing | *Consider silently: How are you being called, like Christ, to compassionate service? Share with one another your call to compassion. If alone, write your response in your journal.*

Listen to or sing a hymn.

All pray: Consoling Spirit of God, come upon this ointment that it may be for us a sign of your presence.

The participants extend both hands over the ointment and in a descending gesture, slowly and silently bring their hands to rest immediately over the ointment. Then all pray the blessing over the ointment.

Loving God,
may this ointment strengthen us
in our oneness with Christ
in compassionate service.

The anointing rite is done in groups of two; each pair receives a small amount of ointment in a small decorative plate or jar. Four areas of the body should be anointed: the head, eyes, hands, and feet. The anointing is done with a partner. One partner assumes the role of anointer and follows the entire rite, and then the rite is repeated with the other partner doing the anointing. Before each area of the body is anointed, the scriptural passage and prayer are read.

Prayer (for head)

Wake up!
Sleepers, rise up from the dead.
Jesus Christ shines on you.

(Ephesians 5:14)

Loving God,
as the head of our sister (brother) is anointed,
may she (he), like Lazarus,
be awakened to new consciousness of Christ.

With a careful, caring motion, those anointing bless the heads of their partners.

Prayer (for eyes)

Those are blessed
who see what you are seeing.
Prophets and rulers wanted to see
what you have seen,
but never did.

(Luke 10:23–24)

Loving God,
as our eyes are anointed
may we, like Martha,
recognize Jesus' presence in the here and now.

*Those anointing gently and carefully bless with oil the area
around each eye of their partner.*

Prayer (for hands)

"Before you stands God's servant," said Mary.
"Let it be just as you have told me."

(Luke 1:38)

Loving God,
as our hands are anointed
may we be empowered
to serve others with love
like true disciples.

Those anointing bless with oil the hands of their partners.

Prayer (for feet)

The feet of the messenger
who announces peace
are beautiful on the mountain.

(Isaiah 52:7)

Loving God,
as our feet are anointed
may we be renewed in our dedication
to follow in the path of Christ,
surrendering our life in loving others.

Those anointing tenderly anoint the feet of their partners.
Partners reverse roles and repeat the entire ritual.

Let us only believe.   **Closing**
May we believe the harder and the more despairingly
as reality seems the more threatening and irreducible.
And then, little by little
we shall see the universal horror relax, and smile at us,
and enfold us in more-than-human hands.

(Teilhard de Chardin)

Materials needed. A cross, a beautiful jar of perfumed   **Setting**
ointment (body lotion), a tablecloth, a Bible, and small
dishes or jars for distribution to each pair of the participants

Suggested music. "I Have Been Anointed," by the
Dameans

Note. Some people have allergic or asthmatic reactions
to perfume. The leader should check with the participants to be sure that this ritual will not be harmful to
anyone.

23
The Service of Love

Call to
Prayer | Be still within and without.
Center yourself in God who loves you.

Reading | As the celebration of Passover approached,
Jesus knew that the time had come at last
for him to leave this world.
He loved his followers
and would until the very end.
Jesus and his friends sat down to supper.
Even Judas who would betray him was there.
Jesus, knowing that he came from God
and would soon be returning,
rose from the meal,
stripped off his outer garments and,
wrapping a towel around his waist,
poured water in a basin.
Then he washed the disciples' feet,
and dried them with the towel.

(John 13:1–5)

Prayer | I've come to think that the only, the supreme, prayer
we can offer up, during these hours
when the road before us is shrouded in darkness,
is that of our Master on the cross:
"Into your hands I commend my spirit."
To the hands that broke and gave life to the bread,
that blessed and caressed, that were pierced; . . .
to the kindly and mighty hands that reach down
to the very marrow of the soul—that mould and create—

to the hands through which so great a love is
transmitted—
it is to these that it is good to surrender our soul,
above all when we suffer or are afraid.
And in so doing there is a great happiness and great
merit.

(Teilhard de Chardin)

One of the participants takes the basin, pitcher, and towel, | **Rite of**
and kneels to wash and dry the feet of another participant. | **Foot**
The person whose feet have been washed then washes the | **Washing**
feet of another participant. This is repeated until all of the
participants have had their feet washed. While the foot
washing is in process, meditative music like "Ubi Caritas" is
played.

Jesus asked, | **Reading**
"Can you comprehend what
I have done for you?"

(John 13:13)

Faith-sharing	*Silently consider your experience of having your feet washed. Were you willing and eager or resistant? Share with one another how this symbolic washing of your feet might serve as a force for your own healing? How does it invite you to be more loving of others?*
Reading	Having washed their feet and dressed again, Jesus sat back down at the table. He asked them again, "Can you comprehend what I have done for you? You proclaim me Lord, and that I am. Now if I am Lord and have washed your feet, you should wash each other's feet, too. I provided this example so that you can imitate me. Disciples are not more important than their leaders. Messengers are not greater than those who send them." <div align="right">(John 13:12–16)</div>
Closing	*Sing or listen to a final hymn.*
Setting	**Materials needed.** A table attractively arranged with a cloth, a Bible, a candle, a basin, a pitcher of water, and towels **Suggested music.** "Ubi Caritas," *Laudate: Music of Taizé,* "Song of the Lord's Supper," by Michael Joncas, "Jesu, Jesu," Ghana folk song translated by Tom Colvin

24
The Paradox of Betrayal

Be still within and without.
Center yourself in the God of forgiveness.

Call to Prayer

The lighted incense is used to bless the crucifix and Bible. During the readings and reflection times, play background meditative music.

Incensing

Jesus asked Peter, "Are you sleeping?
Aren't you strong enough
to stay awake even one hour?"

(Mark 14:37)

Reading

Betrayal is a key mystery in the story of Jesus.
(Adapted from Jean Houston)

Reflection time

Jesus asked Judas,
"Are you really going to betray me
with a kiss?"

(Luke 22:48)

Reading

Trust always contains the seeds of its own betrayal. . . .
It was the close relationships that more often than not
carried the fullest agony of betrayal. . . .

(Houston)

Reflection time

Reading	Jesus told Peter, "The truth is that before the rooster crows in the morning, you will have denied you knew me three times." <div align="right">(Matthew 26:34)</div> Betrayal allows for the coming of reflection and therefore consciousness. . . . The message of betrayal is always that things are much more than they seem. <div align="right">(Houston)</div>

 Reflection time

Reading	Jesus cried out loudly, "My God, my God, why have you deserted me?" <div align="right">(Matthew 27:47)</div> In each of [the] betrayals Jesus is forced to the terrible awareness of having been let down, failed, left alone. . . . At the end of primal trust, Jesus is available to the fullness of the human condition. <div align="right">(Houston)</div>

 Reflection time

Faith-sharing	*Consider: How do you experience the "Judas" or the "Peter" in yourself? How is self-doubt a betrayal of your true self? Have you been betrayed? left alone? Has your ability to love been expanded by your betrayals of other people and their betrayals of you? How is the experience of betrayal your participation in the cross of Christ?* *Share your reflection on these questions with one another. If you are praying alone, write your response in your journal.*

After the incense is lit and the cross incensed, play "Jesus, Remember Me." Each person is invited to reverence the cross by bowing, touching, or kissing the cross and praying these words from the Easter Vigil: "O happy fault . . . which gained for us so great a Redeemer!"

Jesus prayed,
"Forgive them,
they do not understand what they have done."

(Luke 23:34)

The key to redeeming our betrayals is forgiveness. . . .
When this forgiveness is fully known
and experienced in the soul,
you can recognize the "betrayer"
as the instrument of the Larger Story.

(Houston)

Pray or sing the Lord's Prayer.

Rite of Reverencing the Cross

Reading

Closing

Setting | **Materials needed.** A crucifix, a Bible, incense, a censer, all arranged on a table, and matches

Suggested music. "Stay Here," and "Remember Me," *Laudate: Music of Taizé*

Note. Some people have allergic or asthmatic reactions to incense. The leader should check with the participants to be sure that this ritual will not be harmful to anyone.

25
Rose and Thorns

Be still within and without.
Image God's love as a rose unfolding and enfolding you.
Center yourself in this love.

Call to Prayer

Soft meditative music may be played during the reading of the poem.

Reading

I see His blood upon the rose
And in the stars the glory of His eyes,
His body gleams amid eternal snows,
His tears fall from the skies.

I see His face in every flower;
The thunder and the singing of the birds
Are but His voice—and carven by His power
Rocks are His written words.

All pathways by His feet are worn,
His strong heart stirs the ever-beating sea,
His crown of thorns is twined with every thorn,
His cross is every tree.

(Joseph M. Plunkett)

Reflection time. *Contemplate the rose with its thorns.*

Pilate gave orders that Jesus was to be flogged.
The guards formed a crown of thorns,
roughly put it on his head,
and draped him with a purple robe.
They addressed him mockingly,

Reading

"All hail, king of the Jews!"
Then they slapped Jesus in the face.

(John 19:1–3)

 Reflection time

Prayer

Jesus,
we see the scene, we hear the words.
The soldiers mock you
and paradoxically it is in their cruelty
that the truth is proclaimed.
Christ,
you are the reconciler of all that divides and separates.
Let us rest in the awareness and peace
that you are the centering force
that reconciles all that is opposite in us.
Centered in you, we are centered in truth.

Faith-sharing

Silently consider: How do you experience the pull of opposites within you? In what concrete way does it affect your life choices? Is your hope and desire that Christ could be the reconciler of these opposite forces within you?

Share with one another something of your daily struggle with the tug of opposites within you and your prayer and effort toward reconciliation of these opposites. If alone, write your response in your journal.

Rite of the Rose and Thorns

During this time, play gentle background music. The leader invites each participant, in turn, to receive the rose with its thorns, saying, "Receive the rose with thorns as a symbol of paradox and reconciliation. May it be a sign, also, of the bittersweet experience of your own Christian journey."

Upon receiving the rose, please offer a spontaneous prayer that the struggle of opposites within you be reconciled. Please try to be as explicit as you can in naming that which you are most aware of at this time.

Sing a final hymn.

Materials needed. A wreath of branches with thorns arranged on a red cloth, a long-stemmed red rose with thorns, a Bible, and a candle

Suggested music. "Were You There?" or "O Sacred Head Surrounded"

26
The Last Hours

*The room is darkened. In the center, a crucifix and three
lighted candles are arranged on a table.*

**Call to
Prayer**

Be still within and without.
Contemplate the three lighted candles
shining in the darkness,
symbolic of the last three hours of Christ's Passion.
Center yourself in the presence of the suffering Christ.

Prayer

Jesus, may all that is you flow into me.
May your body and blood
    be my food and drink.
May your passion and death
    be my strength and life.
Jesus, with you at my side
    enough has been given.
May the shelter I seek
    be the shadow of your cross.
Let me not run from the love
    which you offer,
But hold me safe from the forces of evil.
On each of my dyings
    shed your light and your love.
Keep calling to me until that day comes,
When, with your saints,
    I may praise you forever. Amen.

(David L. Fleming)

Bowing his head, Jesus surrendered his spirit.
(John 19:30)

Reading

Pray silently for five minutes. Sing the refrain from "Now We Remain," by David Haas. Extinguish one candle.

Response

Bowing his head, Jesus surrendered his spirit.
(John 19:30)

Reading

Pray silently for five minutes. Sing the refrain from "Now We Remain," by David Haas. Extinguish second candle.

Response

Bowing his head, Jesus surrendered his spirit.
(John 19:30)

Reading

Pray silently for five minutes. Sing the refrain from "Now We Remain," by David Haas. Extinguish third candle.

Response

Reflection time. *In the dark, contemplate the death of Jesus.*

Pass the crucifix from one person to another. As you receive and hold the crucifix, offer a spontaneous prayer of gratitude and love.

Rite of the Cross

Jesus Christ, may your death be my life
and in your dying may I learn how to live.
May your struggles be my rest,
Your human weakness my courage,
Your embarrassment my honor,
Your passion my delight,
Your sadness my joy,
in your humiliation may I be exalted.
In a word, may I find all my blessings in your trials.
Amen.
(Peter Faber)

Closing

Setting | **Materials needed.** A crucifix, three candles, and a Bible

Suggested music. "Now We Remain," by David Haas

27

Symbols of Surrender

*Prior to the prayer service the participants need to be invit-
ed to bring a personal symbol of surrender to Christ, for example, a cross, a stone, a picture of a child.*

Be still within and without.
Center yourself in the God of life.

**Call to
Prayer**

A follower of Jesus, Joseph of Arimathaea,
asked Pilate's permission to bury Jesus' body.
Pilate granted the permission,
so they came and carried it away.

Reading

(John 19:38)

Joseph wrapped the body in a fresh shroud
and placed it in his own newly hewn tomb.

(Matthew 27:59–60)

Reflection time

*Everyone takes turns sharing the meaning of their symbol,
expressing how the symbol represents their experience of surrender to Christ. After each shares, he or she places the symbol next to the crucifix. If alone, write about your experience
of surrendering to Christ.*

**Faith-
sharing**

Nicodemus, the disciple who used to visit Jesus only at
        night,
brought a mixture of myrrh and aloes.

Reading

He helped them bind Jesus' body and the spices in linen
    cloth,
following the Jewish burial customs.

(John 19:39–40)

Rite of New Life	*All bless the spices or potpourri with this prayer.*

Loving and Gracious God,
we call your blessing
upon these fragrant herbs and flowers of the earth.
May they be a sign of the fruitfulness of surrender,
of death issuing forth into new life.
May the bitterness of our sufferings
always be sweetened by the remembrance
of your life, death, burial, and Resurrection.

The potpourri is slowly sprinkled over the cross and symbols of the participants. |
| **Music** | *Sing or listen to the selected music. A designated participant comes forward, removes the purple ribbon from the cross, and replaces it with a loosely woven braid consisting of as many yellow or white ribbons as there are participants.* |
| **Reading** | Listen! My servants will become prosperous,
will grow powerful and rise in everyone's esteem.
After the trials he has endured,
he will see the light and have peace.

(Isaiah 52:13; 53:11) |
| **Music** | *Sing an Alleluia of choice. Each participant receives her or his symbol draped with one of the ribbons that made up the braid. While extending the symbol and ribbon, the leader offers a blessing to each participant: "May you go forward with the joy of new life in Christ."* |
| **Closing** | May all that is Jesus flow into us,
bringing us peace and the fire of his love. Amen. |

May God our creator,
Jesus our brother,
and the Holy Spirit
bless us and ours
and bring us all to eternal life. Amen.

Materials needed. A large cross or crucifix draped with a purple ribbon (three-inch ribbon about a yard long) arranged on or standing by a table; a large basket of sweet-smelling potpourri; a basket at the foot of the table; a loosely woven braid of as many yellow or white ribbons as there are participants (one and one-half inch ribbons, about a yard long); and personal symbols of surrender

Suggested music. "Only This I Want," by Dan Schutte

Note. Some people have allergic or asthmatic reactions to potpourri. The leader should check with the participants to be sure that this ritual will not be harmful to anyone.

28
Celebration of Friendship

Call to Prayer | Be still within and without.
Ponder the image of the Visitation.
Center yourself.

Reading | Mary left for a town in Judah and
walked as quickly as possible through the hills.
When she came to Zechariah's house,
she greeted Elizabeth.
During the greeting,
the child in Elizabeth's womb leapt,
and the Holy Spirit filled her.
Giving a loud shout, she declared:
"Mary, you are the most blessed among women.
And, blessed is the child in your womb.
How do I deserve a visit
from the mother of our Lord?
From the very moment you greeted me,
my child has been leaping for joy in my womb.
Truly blessed are you who had faith
that the vow God made to you would come to fullness."
(Luke 1:39–45)

 Reflection time

Music | *Listen to or sing the selected hymn.*

Silently recall to mind and heart significant friendships. Consider how these friends have believed in you. Share with one another how these friendships have been fulfilling and have caused your heart to leap with joy and surprise. If praying alone, write your reflections. | **Faith-sharing**

Background music is played softly. The leader says: "Like Mary and Elizabeth, let us quietly embrace one another with the words, 'Truly blessed are you who had faith that the vow God made to you would come to fullness.'" *Embrace each other, commemorating all the people who have blessed your life. After all have embraced and returned to their places, the music continues for a brief time.* | **Rite of Embrace**

Listen to the selected hymn. | **Music**

Hail Mary, full of grace! | **Closing**
The Lord is with you;
blessed are you among women,
and blessed is the fruit of your womb, Jesus.
Holy Mary, Mother of God,
pray for us sinners now and
at the hour of our death. Amen.

Materials needed. A Bible, a candle, and a statue or a contemporary icon of the Visitation | **Setting**

Suggested music. "To My Surprise," by Rory Cooney, "Blessed Is She," by Colleen Fulmer

29
All Shall Be Well

Call to Prayer | Be still within and without.
Center yourself in the joy of the risen Christ.

Music | *Sing "All Shall Be Well," by Rufino Zaragoza.*

Reading | My lover sings to me,
"Beloved, come with me.
Come, my beautiful one.
Look, winter has gone.
The rains have finished.
Flowers adorn the earth once again.
The season for singing has come.
Turtledoves' cooing can be heard in the land.
Fig trees show their first buds,
and the vines' blossoms send forth their sweet fragrance.
Beloved, come.
Come, my beautiful one."

(Song of Songs 2:10–13)

 Reflection time

Faith-sharing | *Consider: At this time in your life, what aspects of your life are ending and waiting to be embraced and what new beginnings are longing to emerge? Do you share the conviction that "all shall be well"? Share your reflections. If you are praying alone, write your reflections or give them some expression in drawing, watercoloring, or molding in clay.*

Sing "All Shall Be Well."

Reading:
"Winter has gone. The rains have finished."
We have passed through death into life.
Symbolically, let us gently wash away
all stain of tears from each other's face.
As we do this, let us say the words of the Song of Songs,
the "Winter has gone. The rains have finished."

*Each participant takes the crystal goblet filled with water
and the small towel, dips his or her fingers into the water,
turns to the next person, and gently washes and dries the
cheeks of the person while softly repeating the words: "Winter has gone. The rains have finished." He or she then
hands the goblet to the next participant, who in turn ap-
proaches the next person. This continues until all have participated.*

Sing "All Shall Be Well."

"Our good Lord answered
to all the questions and doubts
which I could raise, saying:
I may make all things well,
and I can make all things well,
and I shall make all things well,
and I will make all things well;
and you will see yourself
that every kind of thing will be well.
And in these . . . words
God wishes us to be enclosed
in rest and in peace."
Let us leave in silence,
savoring within our hearts
the sacred touch of our time together.

(Julian of Norwich)

Setting | **Materials needed.** A Bible open to the Song of Songs, a crystal goblet filled with water, a small towel, and a lighted candle, all arranged on an attractive cloth

Suggested music. "All Shall Be Well," by Rufino Zaragoza

30
Bread of Life

Relax. Be still within and without.
Become conscious of your breathing.
Breathe out your distractions and darkness.
Breathe in the light of God's love and presence.
Breathe in and out slowly and deeply.
Center yourself in Christ.

Call to Prayer

Sing the opening hymn. During the singing, the Easter bread is brought in and reverently placed in the center of the table.

Music

As they came nearer to the village of Emmaus
where they were staying the night,
Jesus moved as if to walk on,
but his companions urged him to remain with them.
"Look, night is falling. Stay with us."
So Jesus stayed.
As they sat at the table,
Jesus lifted up the bread and blessed it,
then broke it, and handed it to them.
Suddenly their eyes were opened,
and they recognized him.
But he disappeared.
In great excitement, they declared to each other,
"Weren't our hearts burning inside us
as he explained the Scriptures to us
while we were walking on the road!"

(Luke 24:28–32)

Reading

Music	*Sing the selected song.*
	Reflection time
Faith-sharing	*Bring to mind a new person you have met within the past few weeks. Consider how the time you have spent with that person has been nurturing for you. What does this meeting have to say to you about the presence of Christ in your everyday life? What does it have to say about your call to be Christ in our world? Share with one another your feelings about the meeting with the former stranger. If alone, express your response in your journal.*
Rite of the Easter Bread	*A reader recites the passage from the Scriptures; all respond with the prayer.*

Don't you know that just a pinch of yeast leavens a large batch of dough? (1 Corinthians 5:6)

All: Loving God, make us a nurturing bread for our hungry world.

Discard the old yeast, so that you can be new dough, even unleavened like you are. (1 Corinthians 5:7)

All: Loving God, make us a nurturing bread for our hungry world.

Christ, our Passover, has been sacrificed. (1 Corinthians 5:7)

All: Loving God, make us a nurturing bread for our hungry world.

Let us celebrate the feast not with the old yeast of sin and destruction, but only with the unleavened bread of honesty and truth. (1 Corinthians 5:8)

All: Loving God, make us a nurturing bread for our hungry world.

All bless the Easter bread.

Loving God, we ask your blessing upon this Easter bread.

May it be for those of us who receive it
a remembrance of how, throughout history,
you have been everlastingly faithful in your care.
You gave manna in the desert;
you fed Elijah when he was weary.
Your son, Jesus, gave himself to us as the bread of life.
May this Easter bread be a sign
of our companionship and oneness
with Jesus and with one another.

Let us share our Easter bread.

While all partake of the bread, play background music.

Sing the final hymn.

Closing

Materials needed. A Bible open to chapter 24 of Luke, a candle, and Easter bread arranged on a cloth (Many recipe books have recipes for various ethnic Easter breads, if a member of the group is disposed to baking.)

Suggested music. For background music, "Ave Verum Corpus," by Mozart; "Taste and See," by James E. Moore, "In the Breaking of the Bread," by Bob Hurd, "I Am the Bread of Life," by Suzanne Toolan, or "Panis Angelicus"

Setting

31
Teach Me to Listen

Call to Prayer
Be still within and without.
Be aware of the gift of hearing.
Listen to the sounds and silence around you.
Center yourself in God who speaks to your heart.

Music
Sing or listen to the hymn chosen.

Reading
During the sixth month, God sent Gabriel
to Nazareth in Galilee, to a virgin named Mary
who was betrothed to Joseph of David's line.
Gabriel told Mary,
"Have joy because God favors you, Mary.
God is with you."
Shaken by these words,
Mary wondered what the words meant.
Then Gabriel told her.
"Don't be afraid, Mary. God loves you.
Listen, you will conceive a son.
Name him Jesus.
He will be a person of power
and will be called Son of God.
He will rule the House of Jacob forever."
Mary replied,
"But, how can this be, I do not know man?"
The angel answered, "The Holy Spirit will come upon
        you.
The Most High's power will cover you.
The child will be holy, the Son of God.
Not only that, but your cousin Elizabeth

has conceived a son in her advanced age.
Even though she was thought barren,
she has been pregnant for six months.
For God, nothing is impossible."
Mary answered, "I am God's servant.
Let it be with me as you have said."

(Luke 1:26–38)

Prayer

Dear God, teach us to listen as Mary listened.
Teach me to listen, O God, to those nearest me,
my family, my friends, my coworkers.
Help me to be aware that no matter what words I hear,
the message is, "Accept the person I am. Listen to me."

Reflection time

Prayer

Teach me to listen, my caring God,
to those far from me—
the whisper of the hopeless, the plea of the forgotten,
the cry of the anguished.

Reflection time

Prayer

Teach me to listen, O God my Mother, to myself.
Help me to be less afraid to trust the voice inside—
in the deepest part of me.

Reflection time

Prayer

Teach me to listen, Holy Spirit,
for your voice—
in busyness and in boredom,
in certainty and in doubt,
in noise and in silence.
Teach me, [O God], to listen. Amen.

(John Veltri)

Reflection time

Faith-sharing *Silently recall a word that was transforming for you. Was it a word of encouragement or criticism? Was it a word of instruction or a request? How open were you to listening to this word? Share this word with one another and explain how it was transforming. If alone, write your response in your journal.*

Rite of Anointing of the Ear *One of the participants lifts the perfume vial in a prayerful gesture. All read the prayer of blessing.*

Saint Paul tells us that to God
we are the fragrance of Christ,
the fragrance of life leading to life.
Gracious God, we ask your blessing upon this perfume.
May its fragrance bless our ears
and always call us to be attentive to your Word.
Free us from the fears that block our openness.
Quicken in us a Mary-like responsiveness
to the many ways you speak to us each day. Amen.

Anoint one another's ears with the blessed perfume, while praying, "Blessed are the people who hear God's word and then put it into action" (Luke 8:21).

Prayer Thanks be to God
who always gives us in Christ
a share in his new life,
and through us is spreading everywhere
the fragrance of the word of God. Amen.

Closing *Sing the concluding hymn.*

Materials needed. A Bible, a candle, and a vial of perfume

Suggested music. "We Have Been Told," by David Haas

Note. Some people have allergic or asthmatic reactions to perfume. The leader should check with the participants to be sure that this ritual will not be harmful to anyone.

32
The Easter Egg

Prior to this prayer service, ask the participants to bring an Easter egg decorated in a way that makes the egg symbolic for them.

Call to Prayer

Be still within and without.
Be centered in the joy of the Risen Christ.

Music

Open the celebration with a joyous song.

Faith-sharing

Each participant shares what his or her Easter egg symbolizes. After sharing, each one places his or her egg in the Easter basket on the table. If alone, write about the symbolism of your Easter egg in your journal.

Reading

The egg is very appropriate in this context since it is symbolic of new life and the capacity for giving birth. The colored egg is also associated with Astarte, goddess of spring, from whose name our word "Easter" is derived. Colored eggs were used in the spring celebrations honoring the goddess, as they are today at Easter. (Nancy Qualls-Corbett)

Mary Magdalene, who is so prominent in the Resurrection passages, is also associated with the Easter egg.

There are myths which depict Mary Magdalene's ability to perform miracles. One tells of when she saw and spoke to the risen Christ, as it is believed she was the first to do. She hurried off to tell the other disciples. On her way, she met Pontius Pilate and told him of the wondrous news.

"Prove it," Pilate said. At that moment a woman carrying a basket of eggs passed by and Mary Magdalene took one in her hand. As she held it up before Pilate, the egg turned a brilliant red. To attest to the legendary event, in the cathedral which bears her name in Jerusalem there stands a beautiful statue of Mary Magdalene holding a colored egg. (Qualls-Corbett)

Sing an Alleluia. **Music**

Reading

Mary Magdalene stood near the tomb weeping.
When she looked inside, two angels in white
sat where Jesus' body had been.
They asked her, "Why are you weeping?"
"They have taken Jesus away!
I don't know where they have taken him."
Then, turning around, Mary saw Jesus standing nearby,
but she did not recognize him.
"Woman," Jesus asked, "why are you crying?
Who are you searching for?"
Thinking that Jesus was the gardener, she said,
"Sir, please, tell me where you put his body
if you have carried him away."
"Mary," Jesus said.
At which, Mary replied, "Master!"
"Now do not hold onto me, Mary,
because I have yet to ascend!
Go tell my sisters and brothers that
I am ascending to our God."
Mary rushed back and told the disciples,
"I have seen the Lord!"
(John 20:11–18)

In the spirit of this Gospel reading, spend a few moments con- **Rite of**
templating the basket of Easter eggs. Breathe in the beauty **Dance**
of the eggs and the promise of all that they symbolize.

99

Listen to the verses and sing the refrain to "Mary Magdalene's Song," by Colleen Fulmer. Stand for gestures during the refrain.

For the first line, "Praise our God who raises us to new life," slowly raise your right arm.

During the next line, "God who does such wonders," raise your left arm.

On the first Alleluia, lower both arms, and the second Alleluia, raise both arms up.

Right at the end, your fists should be clenched, then burst open with a pulse of energy (adapted from Martha Ann Kirk).

Prayer

Lord Jesus, we ask you now
to help us to remain with you always,
to be close to you with all the ardor of our hearts,
to take up joyfully the mission you entrust to us
and that is to continue your presence
and spread the good news of your Resurrection.

(Carlo Maria Martini)

Closing

God of Promise,
continue always to keep alive in our heart
the joy of Jesus risen.
Bless these eggs,
symbolic of your promise of new life
continually being birthed within us. Amen.

The participants take their eggs home.

Setting

Materials needed. A Bible open to chapter 20 of John, a lighted candle, and an Easter basket with balloons, flowers, grass, and one egg colored red

Suggested music. "Mary Magdalene's Song," by Colleen Fulmer, "Sing a New Song," by Dan Schutte

33
Our Story

Be still within and without.
Center yourself in the God of history.

Call to Prayer

Loving and gracious God,
you have placed in our heart
a marvelous capacity for remembering.
You are a God of history—
a history filled with light and darkness.
Help us to remember your story and our own,
and in the remembering,
fill us with gratitude and joy. Amen.

Prayer

Sing one verse of the chosen hymn.

Music

Allow your heart to remember a special moment of being loved and a moment of being truly loving, a time when you were particularly vulnerable and a time when you extended yourself.

Reflection

Sing another verse of the song.

Music

Jesus always used parables with the people.
In doing so, he fulfilled the prophecy that said,
"I will speak to you using parables
and thus reveal what has been obscure
since time began."

Reading

(Matthew 13:34–35)

Rite of Storytelling | *The Bible is transferred from the storytelling chair to a nearby table or stand.*

Jesus shared his life through the stories he told, through parables. Recall again your moment of being loved or loving truly, and when you are ready, come forward and sit in the storytelling chair. When someone comes forward to tell their story the ribbons on the chair are draped over their shoulders.

Share your story, your parable of a time when you experienced love and loving. After you have told your story remove a ribbon from the chair.

Music | *Sing one or two more verses of the song.*

Closing | The Word of life
that has existed from the creation
that you have heard and seen
and observed and touched:
this is our subject.

(1 John 1:1)

Setting | **Materials needed**. A chair (the back of it tied with streamers of different colored ribbons on either side), a Bible opened to Matthew 13:34–35 resting on the beribboned storytelling chair draped with a twelve-inch ribbon for each participant

Suggested music. "Song of the Body of Christ," and "We Have Been Told," by David Haas

Note. The participants should know one another fairly well before entering into this service.

34
Welcoming the Light

The room is darkened. All stand to welcome the light of Christ, as one of the participants carries a large candle to the center of the room. A second participant incenses the candle.

Be centered in Christ.

Call to Prayer

I am the light of the world;
those who follow me will not be walking in the dark;
they will have the light of life.

(John 8:12)

Reading

Reflection time

Sing the opening song.

Music

Rite of Sharing Light | *Form a circle around the large candle. Each participant holds an unlit candle. Each is invited in turn to come forward to light her or his candle from the large candle as a sign of sharing the light of the risen Christ.*

After a participant lights his or her candle, all the other participants name a "resurrection quality" they experience in the person who has lit the candle. The quality may be how they have been supported, inspired, or consoled by this person or it may be a particular quality of his or her personality. The lighting proceeds slowly until all have lit the candles and have been affirmed.

Closing | *Play and sing "The Lord Is My Light." Sway gently with the rhythm of the music. Softly sing the refrain. After the music, all participants leave in silence, taking their candles with them, and carrying in their hearts the tender light of this time together.*

Setting | **Materials needed.** A Bible opened to John 8:12, a large candle on a lovely cloth (possibly the paschal candle if it is available), if available use Ted DeGrazia's picture of the Resurrection: "Little Angel Guarding Christ as an Infant," a small candle for each participant, a censer, incense, charcoal, and matches

Suggested music. "The Lord Is My Light," *Laudate: Music of Taizé,* or "Psalm 27: The Lord Is My Light," by David Haas

Note. Some people have allergic or asthmatic reactions to incense. The leader should check with the participants to be sure that this ritual will not be harmful to anyone.

Index of Themes

Resources

Ahlers, Julia, Rosemary Broughton, and Carl Koch, comps. *Womenpsalms*. Winona, MN: Saint Mary's Press, 1992.

Bergan, Jacqueline Syrup, and S. Marie Schwan. The Take and Receive Series: *Love, Forgiveness, Birth, Surrender, Freedom*. Winona, MN: Saint Mary's Press, 1985–88.

Gabriele, Edward. *Act Justly, Love Tenderly, Walk Humbly: Prayers for Peace and Justice*. Winona, MN: Saint Mary's Press, 1995.

Kirk, Martha Ann. *Celebrations of Biblical Women's Stories*. Kansas City, MO: Sheed and Ward, 1987.

Koch, Carl, and Michael Culligan, comps. *Open Hearts, Helping Hands: Prayers by Lay Volunteers in Mission*. Winona, MN: Saint Mary's Press, 1993.

Morneau, Robert. *Gift, Mystery, and Calling: Prayers and Reflections*. Winona, MN: Saint Mary's Press, 1994.

Mossi, John, and Suzanne Toolan. *Canticles and Gathering Prayers*. Winona, MN: Saint Mary's Press, 1989.

Simsic, Wayne. *Garden Prayers: Planting the Seeds of Your Inner Life*. Winona, MN: Saint Mary's Press, 1995.

Acknowledgments (*continued*)

The scriptural quotations throughout this book are freely adapted and are not to be interpreted or used as official translations of the Scriptures.

The psalms quoted in this book are from *Psalms Anew: In Inclusive Language*, compiled by Nancy Schreck and Maureen Leach (Winona, MN: Saint Mary's Press, 1986). Copyright © 1986 by Saint Mary's Press. All rights reserved.

The excerpts on pages 39–40 and 81 by Peter Faber, "Prayer for Detachment" and "From Death to Life," are from *Hearts on Fire: Praying with Jesuits*, collected and edited by Michael Harter (Saint Louis: Institute of Jesuit Sources, 1993), pages 25 and 70. Copyright © 1993 by the Institute of Jesuit Sources. Used with permission.

The excerpt on page 41 by Pierre Teilhard de Chardin, "Enfold Me in Your Heart," is from *The Divine Milieu*. Copyright © 1957 Editions du Seuil, Paris. English translation copyright © 1960 by William Collins Sons and Company, London, and Harper and Row, Publishers, New York. Renewed © 1988 by Harper and Row, Publishers. Reprinted by permission of the publishers.

The excerpts on page 50 by Caryll Houselander are from *The Mother of Christ* (London: A. Wheaton and Company, 1986), pages 17, 7, and 32. Copyright © 1978 by H. J. Tayler. Reprinted by permission of Sheed and Ward. To order, call 800-333-7373.

The excerpt on page 51 by Caryll Houselander is from *The Reed of God* (London: Sheed and Ward, 1976), page 34. Copyright © 1944 by Caryll Houselander.

The adaptation on pages 53–54 by Basil Pennington is from *Call to the Center: The Gospel's Invitation to Deeper Prayer* (New York: Doubleday, 1990), page 24. Copyright © 1990 by Cistercian Abbey of Spencer. Used by permission of Doubleday, a division of Bantam Doubleday Dell Publishing Group.

The excerpts on pages 55 and 56 by Meister Eckhart, Julian of Norwich, and Hildegard of Bingen are from *Original Blessing* by Matthew Fox (Santa Fe, NM: Bear and Company, 1983), pages 81, 82, and 81, respectively. Copyright © 1983 by Bear and Company.

The excerpts on pages 59–60 and 80 by David L. Fleming, "Soul of Christ," are from *The Spiritual Exercises: A Literal Translation and a Contemporary Reading*. Copyright © 1978 by the Institute of Jesuit Sources. Used with permission.

The excerpt on page 63 by Pierre Teilhard de Chardin is from *The Heart of the Matter*, translated by René Hague (New York: Harcourt Brace Jovanovich, 1978), pages 121–122. Copyright © 1978 by William Collins and Company and Harcourt Brace Jovanovich.

The excerpt on page 69 by Pierre Teilhard de Chardin is from *Teilhard de Chardin on Love and Suffering*, by Paul Chauchard (New York: Paulist Press Deus Books, 1966), page 7. Copyright © 1966 by the Missionary Society of Saint Paul the Apostle in the State of New York.

The excerpt on pages 70–71 by Pierre Teilhard de Chardin, "Entrusting Myself to the Hands of Jesus," is quoted from Harter, *Hearts on Fire*, page 72. Copyright © 1993. Used with permission.

The excerpts on pages 73, 74, and 75 by Jean Houston are from *The Search for the Beloved: Journeys in Sacred Psychology* (New York: St. Martin's Press, 1987), pages 114, 115, and 117. Copyright © 1987 by Jean Houston. Reprinted by permission of the Putnam Publishing Group and Jeremy P. Tarcher.

The excerpt on page 77 by Joseph M. Plunkett is from *Christian Prayer* (New York: Catholic Book Publishing Company, 1976), page 2060. Copyright © 1976 by the International Committee on English in the Liturgy.

The excerpt on page 89 by Julian of Norwich is from *Julian of Norwich: Showings*, translated by Edmund Colledge and James Walsh (New York: Paulist Press, 1978), page 22, from the Classics of Western Spirituality series. Copyright © 1978 by the Missionary Society of Saint Paul the Apostle in the State of New York.

The excerpt on page 95 by John Veltri, "Teach Me to Listen," is quoted in Harter, *Hearts on Fire*, page 21. Originally published in *Orientations*, vol. 1. Copyright © 1993 by Loyola House. Used with permission of the author.

The excerpts on pages 98–99 by Nancy Qualls-Corbett are from *The Sacred Prostitute: Eternal Aspect of the Feminine* (Toronto: Inner City Books, 1988), pages 150–151. Copyright © 1988 by Nancy Qualls-Corbett. Used with permission of the publisher.

The excerpts on page 100 by Colleen Fulmer, "Mary Magdalene's Song," are from *Celebrations of Biblical Women's Stories: Tears, Milk, and Honey*, by Martha Ann Kirk (Kansas City, MO: Sheed and Ward, 1987), pages 108–109. Copyright © 1987 by Martha Ann Kirk. Reprinted by permission of Sheed and Ward. To order, call 800-333-7373.

The excerpt on page 100 by Carlo Maria Martini, "Help Us to Remain Close to You" is from *Journeying with the Lord* (Staten Island, NY: Alba House, 1987). Copyright © 1987 by Alba House. Used with permission of the publisher.

Other books by
Jacqueline Syrup Bergan and Marie Schwan
available from Saint Mary's Press:

The Take and Receive series is based on the spiritual exercises of Saint Ignatius. Each volume is similarly struc-
tured: daily meditations are centered on the theme of the
book for each of the six weeks in the cycle. Each day's
prayer begins with a scriptural passage and includes an in-
sightful commentary and a suggested approach to the
day's reflection.

> **Birth,** ISBN 0-88489-170-4, 6¾ x 8, 154 pages,
> paper, $6.95
>
> **Forgiveness,** ISBN 0-88489-169-0, 6¾ x 8, 166
> pages, paper, $6.95
>
> **Freedom,** ISBN 0-88489-172-0, 6¾ x 8, 161 pages,
> paper, $6.95
>
> **Love,** ISBN 0-88489-168-2, 6¾ x 8, 128 pages,
> paper, $6.95
>
> **Surrender,** ISBN 0-88489-171-2, 6¾ x 8, 153 pages,
> paper, $6.95

Leader's guides for each of the Take and Receive books
are available from Saint Mary's Press for $6.95 each.

Praying with Ignatius of Loyola (ISBN 0-88489-
263-8, 6 x 9, 117 pages, paper, $6.95) is one of the books
in the very popular Companions for the Journey series. It
contains a brief biography of Ignatius, an outline of his
major spiritual themes, and fifteen meditations based on
his thoughts and writings.